A Note to Parents and Teachers

DK READERS is a compelling program for beginning readers, designed in conjunction with literacy experts, including Maureen Fernandes, B.Ed (Hons). Maureen has spent many years teaching literacy, both in the classroom and as a consultant in schools.

Beautiful illustrations and superb full-colour photographs combine with engaging, easy-to-read stories to offer a fresh approach to each subject in the series.

Each DK READER is guaranteed to capture a child's interest while developing his or her reading skills, general knowledge and love of reading.

The five levels of DK READERS are aimed at different reading abilities, enabling you to choose the books that are exactly right for your child:

Pre-level 1: Learning to read
Level 1: Beginning to read
Level 2: Beginning to read alone
Level 3: Reading alone
Level 4: Proficient readers

The "normal" age at which a child begins to read can be anywhere from three to eight years old. Adult participation through the lower levels is very helpful for providing encouragement, discussing storylines and sounding out unfamiliar words.

No matter which level you select, you can be sure that you are helping your child learn to read, then read to learn!

LONDON, NEW YORK, MUNICH,
MELBOURNE, AND DELHI

Editor Kate Simkins
Designers Cathy Tincknell
and John Kelly
Senior Editor Catherine Saunders
Brand Manager Lisa Lanzarini
Publishing Manager Simon Beecroft
Category Publisher Alex Allan
DTP Designer Hanna Ländin
Production Rochelle Talary

Reading Consultant
Maureen Fernandes

Published in Great Britain in 2007 by
Dorling Kindersley Limited,
80 Strand, London WC2R 0RL

Some material contained in this book was previously published in
2006 in *Tales of the Dead: Ancient China*

07 08 09 10 10 9 8 7 6 5 4 3 2 1

A CIP record for this book is available from the British Library.

ISBN: 978-1-40531-837-2

High-res workflow proofed by Media Development
and Printing Ltd, UK.
Design and digital artworking by John Kelly and Cathy Tincknell.
Printed and bound in China by L. Rex Printing Co. Ltd.

All artwork by Inklink except the illustrations of the Great Wall on
page 42, the terracotta soldiers and the town on page 44, the junk
on page 45, the palace on page 46 and the terracotta soldiers on
page 47 by Richard Bonson.

Discover more at
www.dk.com

Contents

DK READERS

PROFICIENT
4
READERS

INSTRUMENTS of DEATH

Written by Stewart Ross
Illustrated by Inklink

INSTRUMENTS OF DEATH

Shen's story takes place in Ancient China about 2,500 years ago. China was ruled by Emperor Shihuangdi, a ruthless warrior who had conquered all the kingdoms of China and united them for the first time under the Qin Empire. Our hero, Shen, lives in a village near the Great Wall of China. Turn to page 42 to see a map and timeline, and then let the story begin....

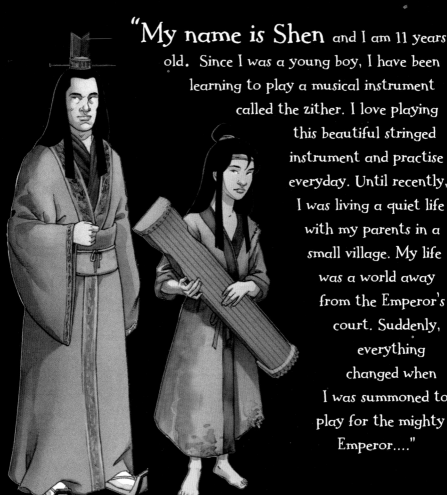

"**My name is Shen** and I am 11 years old. Since I was a young boy, I have been learning to play a musical instrument called the zither. I love playing this beautiful stringed instrument and practise everyday. Until recently, I was living a quiet life with my parents in a small village. My life was a world away from the Emperor's court. Suddenly, everything changed when I was summoned to play for the mighty Emperor...."

IT WAS EVENING IN MY VILLAGE IN NORTHERN CHINA.

I WAS PRACTISING MY MUSIC.

EXCELLENT, SHEN!

MY TEACHERS SAID I HAD GREAT TALENT.

*Words in **bold** appear in the glossary on page 42.*

BUT I WAS LUCKY NOT TO BE TOILING ON THE **GREAT WALL**...

...LIKE OTHERS IN MY VILLAGE.

FASTER, YOU DOGS!

THERE WERE STORIES OF TERRIBLE ACCIDENTS.

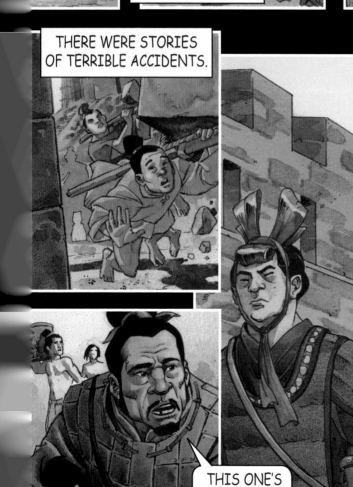

THIS ONE'S DEAD!

OH, NO! ON YOUR KNEES! IT'S THE **EMPEROR**!

DID YOU KNOW? *The Great Wall was built to keep out the Empire's enemie*

HE WAS **SHIHUANGDI**...

...SON OF HEAVEN, LORD OF LIFE...

...AND OF DEATH.

BRING OUT THE **CORRUPT OVERSEERS**!

LET THE **EXECUTIONS** BEGIN!

THE EMPEROR SAW ENEMIES EVERYWHERE...

...AND PUNISHED THEM RUTHLESSLY.

...nishments in Ancient China included death by being buried alive.

DID YOU KNOW? *Ancient Chinese zithers usually had seven strings.*

Shihuangdi became the king of Qin when he was 13 years old.

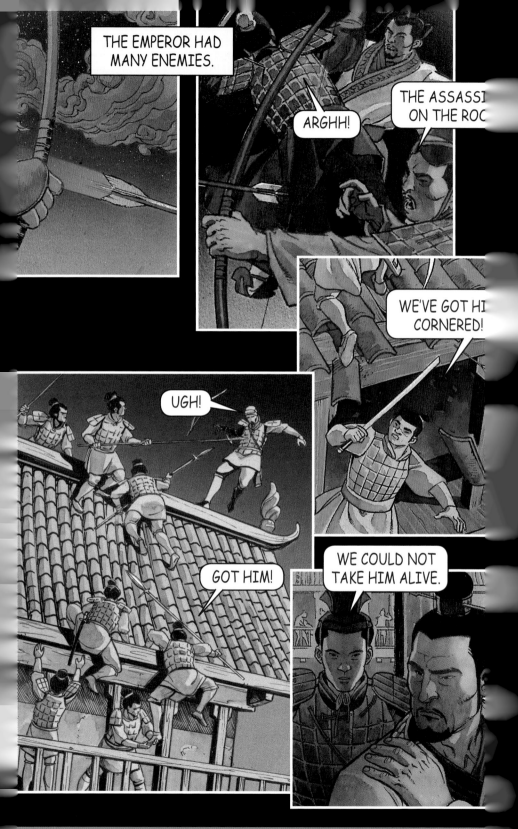

DID YOU KNOW? *"Shihuangdi" means "the first emperor".*

OPEN UP!

THEY CAME TO MY **HOME** IN THE MIDDLE OF THE NIGHT.

IN THE NAME OF THE EMPEROR!

WHY US? WHAT HAVE WE DONE?

WE'VE COME FOR THE BOY!

BUT HE'S DONE NOTHING WRONG!

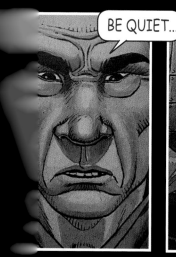

BE QUIET...

...AND YOU WON'T BE HARMED.

THE GUARDS ORDERED ME TO BRING MY ZITHER.

DID YOU KNOW? Most people in Ancient China lived in the countryside

SAVE YOUR TEARS! THE BOY IS WANTED AT COURT.

THEN WE WERE GONE...

...LEAVING MY PARENTS WITH **MONEY** IN PLACE OF A SON.

I WAS TAKEN UNDER HEAVY GUARD TO BEGIN MY NEW LIFE.

They lived as farmers, growing crops such as rice and wheat.

DID YOU KNOW? *The Chinese believed China was the centre of the world*

DID YOU KNOW? *The court was made up of nobles such as dukes and count*

AS I THOUGHT ABOUT THE MYSTERIOUS COUNT GAO, WE ARRIVED AT THE NEAREST PORT.

WE TOOK RIVER **JUNKS**.

THE EMPEROR WENT ABOARD THE LARGEST BOAT.

HE SET SAIL IMMEDIATELY.

FASTER!

WE FOLLOWED IN A SMALLER VESSEL.

DID YOU KNOW? Junks were powered by sails that caught in the wind.

GAO'S BLADE FLASHED IN THE SUNLIGHT.

SUDDENLY, THE RIVER BANK WAS ALIVE WITH PEOPLE!

SMALL BOATS SPED TOWARDS US!

IT COULD ONLY MEAN ONE THING.

DID YOU KNOW? Junks could hold up to 600 tonnes (660 tons) of cargo.

LOOKS LIKE THEY'VE ABANDONED SHIP!

'AIT!

ONE...

TWO...

...THREE! CHARGE!!

GET THEM!

AMBUSH!

RUN!

DID YOU KNOW? Chinese swords were made of bronze or iron.

DID YOU KNOW? *Heavy goods like grain were moved by boat.*

The rich in Ancient China travelled by horse-drawn carriages.

DID YOU KNOW? The Qin palace was in Xianyang in the north.

THE BEAUTY OF THE PALACE SOON SWEPT ALL OTHER THOUGHTS ASIDE.

THE MASTER OF THE ROYAL MUSIC SHOWED ME AROUND.

HURRY UP, BOY!

STOP STARING LIKE A PEASANT!

LATER, AS I TRIED TO PRACTISE...

HOW'S IT GOING?

I THINK I'M DOOMED!

The palace was protected by high walls and heavily guarded gates.

WHY'S THAT?

I'M SO NERVOUS ABOUT PLAYING IN FRONT OF THE WHOLE COURT.

BUT YOU'RE THE EMPEROR'S NEW FAVOURITE.

HUH?

MAYBE THIS WILL HELP YOUR CONFIDENCE.

IT'S THE MOST BEAUTIFUL ZITHER I'VE EVER SEEN!

HOW CAN I EVER THANK YOU?

DID YOU KNOW? *The Chinese invented many things, including paper.*

NO NEED. YOU SAVED MY LIFE.

JUST PLAY WELL.

HOW THOUGHTFUL!

I CAME TO OBSERVE THE TALENTED SHEN.

BUT WHAT A FANTASTIC ZITHER!

LADY MEILING, YOU HONOUR US WITH YOUR PRESENCE!

IS IT FOR THE BOY?

YES, MY LADY!

SUCH WONDERFUL **CRAFTSMANSHIP!**

They also invented fireworks, wheelbarrows and umbrellas.

29

DID YOU KNOW? The dragon was the symbol of the emperor.

TOO WORRIED TO SLEEP, I WENT OUTSIDE.

I STOOD WATCHING THE **STARS**.

ISN'T THAT...

...COUNT GAO?!

I WONDERED WHERE HE WAS GOING SO LATE.

HE DISAPPEARED OUT OF SIGHT.

The Chinese believed dragons brought good luck.

DID YOU KNOW? *Shihuangdi had a magnificent tomb built.*

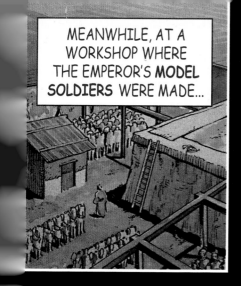

MEANWHILE, AT A WORKSHOP WHERE THE EMPEROR'S **MODEL SOLDIERS** WERE MADE...

MY LORD?

I'VE BROUGHT THE **WEAPON**...

EXCELLENT! GIVE IT TO ME!

BE CAREFUL NOT TO TOUCH THE BLADE.

THE POISON BRINGS INSTANT DEATH!

A huge army of clay model soldiers was made to guard the tomb.

DID YOU KNOW? *Long hair was fashionable for men and women.*

In Ancient China, people used to sleep on the floor.

DID YOU KNOW? *The emperor dressed in fine clothes made of silk.*

SILENCE! HOW DARE YOU INSULT ME WITH THIS DIN!

I'LL DEAL WITH YOU AFTER THE **CEREMONY**!

POOR BOY!

HA! WHAT A FOOL!

THE NOBLES BEGAN **PAYING HOMAGE** TO THE MIGHTY EMPEROR.

GAO WENT FIRST, LOOKING AS SINISTER AS EVER.

I **SUBMIT** TO YOUR GREATNESS, O EMPEROR OF THE WORLD!

He wore elaborate headdresses to make himself look important.

DID YOU KNOW? *Silk cloth was first made in Ancient China.*

It is made from threads spun by silkworms, a type of caterpillar.

DID YOU KNOW? The Chinese Empire ended in 1912.

WAS HE REALLY A **TRAITOR**?

YES! HE WAS A CHU **SPY**.

I HAVE BEEN WATCHING HI... FOR MONTHS

GAO, YOU HAVE SERVED ME WELL!

AS HAVE YOU, SHEN!

YOU SEEM TO BRING ME LUCK!

I THINK I'LL KEEP YOU CLOSE AT HAND.

FRIENDS?

NEVER!

TH... EN...

It had lasted longer than any other empire in the world.

 King Menes unites Egypt
c. 3100

 Minoan civilisation develops on Crete
c. 2000

 Zhou dynasty starts in China
c. 1050

3000 BCE (BEFORE COMMON ERA)   2000 BCE   1000 BCE

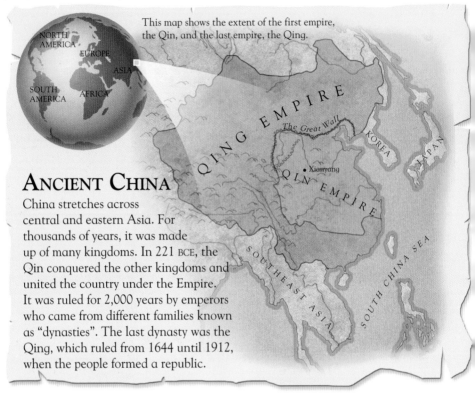

This map shows the extent of the first empire, the Qin, and the last empire, the Qing.

ANCIENT CHINA

China stretches across central and eastern Asia. For thousands of years, it was made up of many kingdoms. In 221 BCE, the Qin conquered the other kingdoms and united the country under the Empire. It was ruled for 2,000 years by emperors who came from different families known as "dynasties". The last dynasty was the Qing, which ruled from 1644 until 1912, when the people formed a republic.

GLOSSARY

EMPEROR   PAGE 6

The emperor was the ruler of the Chinese Empire. The First Emperor, Shihuangdi, conquered many Chinese kingdoms to create the Empire.

GREAT WALL   PAGE 6

The Great Wall of China was built to protect the Empire from foreign invaders in the north. Shihuangdi joined up the existing small walls to create the Great Wall. It was added to and rebuilt over hundreds of years.

Most of the original Qin wall was rebuilt in stone by later emperors

The Great Wall being built

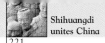
Shihuangdi unites China
221

Rome invaded by barbarians
410

Mongols establish Yuan dynasty in China
1279

US astronauts land on the Moon
1969

TIMELINE

1 CE (COMMON ERA)   1000 CE   2000 CE

YOU ARE HERE

SHIHUANGDI   PAGE 7

Shihuangdi (pronounced She-Her-Wang-Di) was the First Emperor of China. He ruled the Qin (pronounced Chin) kingdom that conquered the other Chinese kingdoms and created the Empire in 221 BCE.

Government minister

Shihuangdi

A Chinese orchestra

A zither being played on a stand

CORRUPT OVERSEERS   PAGE 7

The overseers made sure the building work was done properly. The corrupt ones were dishonest.

EXECUTIONS   PAGE 7

Executions are killing people as a punishment.

ZITHER   PAGE 8

Shen's instrument was a type of zither called a *qin*. It had seven strings and was played on the lap or on a stand. Zithers usually formed part of an orchestra.

ASSASSINS   PAGE 9

People who try to kill a ruler or leader are called assassins. Many assassins tried to kill Shihuangdi because he was a harsh ruler.

These men are to be executed by being buried alive

43

The terracotta soldiers being put in the emperor's tomb

GUARDS PAGE 9

The emperor's many guards protected him from assassins. He even built his own model army to protect him after death. These terracotta (clay) soldiers can still be seen today.

COURT PAGE 11

The court was made up of the noble people who lived with the emperor in his palaces and went with him on his travels. Some of the court has travelled with him to the Great Wall.

CAPITAL PAGE 11

The city where the emperor lived and from which he ruled the Empire was the capital city. In Shihuangdi's time, it was at Xianyang (She-An-Yang) in the north.

HOME PAGE 12

Most people in Ancient China were farmers who lived on crops such as rice. Their homes were small wooden huts with thatched or tiled roofs.

Rice being grown

Farmer's home

A busy Chinese city

MONEY　　　　　　　PAGE 13

At the time of Shihuangdi, Chinese money was in the form of bronze coins. They could be used throughout the Empire. Some coins were shaped like knives and spades.

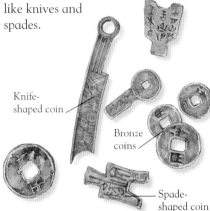

Knife-shaped coin

Bronze coins

Spade-shaped coin

MUSICIAN　　　　　　PAGE 15

Music and musicians were an important part of court life. The court orchestra played when the emperor received visitors or held banquets.

SINISTER　　　　　　PAGE 15

If someone is described as sinister, they look threatening or wicked.

KINGDOM OF CHU　　　PAGE 17

Chu was one of the kingdoms that the Qin defeated to create the Empire. Some of the nobles in Chu were still unhappy about the Qin victory.

JUNKS　　　　　　　PAGE 18

Junks were Chinese wooden sailing ships. They were used to carry goods along rivers and by sea.

A Chinese river junk

Master Swordsman   Page 19

Chinese soldiers used weapons such as swords and spears. A master swordsman was a soldier who was highly skilled at using a blade.

Pirates   Page 21

Pirates are thieves who steal from ships. Attacks by pirates were common in Chinese rivers and seas.

Port   Page 24

A port is a place on a river or coast where boats can load and unload.

Goods being loaded onto boats at a port

Banquet   Page 25

A banquet is a grand party at which lots of food is served. Rich Chinese people, like those at court, ate lots of dishes that included meat, fish, chicken and vegetables. They drank wine made from rice and other grains.

Craftsmanship   Page 29

Something made well by a skilled worker is said to show good craftsmanship. The Chinese were highly skilled at making fine objects from materials like bronze and silk.

Palace   Page 26

The emperor lived in a grand building called a palace. It had a special room called a throne room where the emperor greeted his guests.

Throne room

Model soldier

Worker

Arrows

Spear

Bow

WEAPON   PAGE 33
Chinese weapons included swords, spears, axes and bows. They invented a powerful type of bow called a crossbow and were the first to use gunpowder to make rockets.

OUT OF BOUNDS   PAGE 34
Somewhere that is out of bounds is a place that may only be entered by those with permission.

PAYING HOMAGE   PAGE 37
To pay someone homage means to show them honour and respect. Count Gao, Duke Song and the other nobles bow before the emperor to show that they honour him and that he is their master.

Nobles paying homage to the emperor

CEREMONY   PAGE 37
A ceremony is a special event held to celebrate something, where things are done in a particular way.

SUBMIT   PAGE 37
To submit is to give in to the power of someone else. Count Gao is telling the emperor that he knows he is less powerful than his master.

TRAITOR   PAGE 41
A traitor is someone who betrays their country or ruler. Song has betrayed the emperor by trying to kill him!

SPY   PAGE 41
A spy is someone who watches others secretly to gather information. Spies are often pretending to be someone they are not. Duke Song was pretending to be loyal to the emperor.

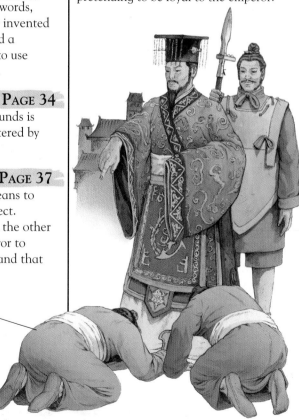